WILD
SOLITUDE

WILD
SOLITUDE

love poems

Lorraine Lipani

JALALA ARTS PRESS

Copyright © 2015 Lorraine Lipani

All rights reserved. No part of this book may be reproduced or transmitted in any form or by any means, electronic or mechanical, including photocopying, recording, or by any information storage and retrieval system, or internet program or system, without written permission from the author.

Book & cover design
Connie King, Constance King Design
ckingdesign.com

Cover art
Karen K. Waller, *Mother Mountain*
© 2015 Karen K. Waller
karenwaller9@gmail.com

Jalala Arts Press
P.O. Box 223
The Sea Ranch, CA 95497
www.jalalaarts.com
jalalaarts@gmail.com

ISBN: 978-0-9968888-0-6
Printed in USA

The poem "Bird Fun" thanks William Carlos William for inspiration: "The Red Wheelbarrow."

For Jolly Smith

It is no small gift to love another.

Introduction

These poems came about in the high desert of New Mexico, where I lived for twenty-five years. My lover and I kept horses on a small ranch in the Rockies, bordering wilderness. Such pristine beauty deepened my appreciation of the natural world, of loving another, and of a spiritual essence palpable in solitude.

As a practice, I write a poem in early morning. Doing so seems to open my heart to the Beauty around me that whispers "Love is all there is."

contents

part one: nature love

3	~	manna
5	~	enchanted
7	~	juniper
9	~	high desert air
11	~	love potion
13	~	grace let loose
15	~	simple life
17	~	all of it is love
19	~	marvel
21	~	winter stream
23	~	chance
25	~	bird fun
27	~	magpies
29	~	snow dance
31	~	spring
33	~	owl
35	~	guests
37	~	seasonal shift
39	~	neighborhood
41	~	purgatory
43	~	o shaman a question
45	~	blue heeler
47	~	dusk
49	~	rainbow
51	~	common tongue
53	~	yin yang

55 ~ peace of heart
57 ~ weather
59 ~ in the middle
61 ~ the sea
63 ~ love song

part two: another love

67 ~ the glance
69 ~ soft welcome
71 ~ bright light
73 ~ a curve of clear water
75 ~ delicate
77 ~ simple magic
79 ~ aloha
81 ~ listening
83 ~ joy
85 ~ charms
87 ~ paradise
89 ~ skin
91 ~ tender
93 ~ pleasure
95 ~ love
97 ~ iridescence
99 ~ bliss
101 ~ younger
103 ~ tracks

part three: wild solitude

107	~	full moon taos
109	~	isn't it the same
111	~	latir
113	~	déjà vu
115	~	bosque del apache
117	~	riding after hummingbird
119	~	persona
121	~	feral
123	~	keep my eye
125	~	aloof
127	~	split second
129	~	intimacy
131	~	upstream
133	~	amazonia
135	~	solstice
137	~	solitude
139	~	curious
141	~	sense of place
143	~	is it kind
145	~	new map
147	~	openly beneficent
149	~	change
151	~	spring run-off
153	~	forgive
155	~	a moment
157	~	champagne
159	~	a bell
161	~	Acknowledgements
163	~	About the author

part one

nature love

manna

some say true love is out of reach
so long as ego-needs
weigh and measure
the returns

I say Love is bigger than that
well-rooted in stars
moonlight-nourished
tapped at the heart
flows freely, impeccably

like a mountain stream whose bed
is surrendered of much soil
for the sake of the sound
the feel of such joy
tumbling over stones

I say Love is the manna in bird song
in the breezes teasing my dreams
like strands of hair across my eyes

enchanted

plant hollyhocks in cool morning earth
slow loving afternoon siesta, then
ride horses in sage-scented breeze

high desert to my surprise
keeps me in essentials
aphrodisia, delight and joy
count me a woman with her heart
flung open

most days I make pots
half-smile and soft eyes
clay-woman flies as if
here, earth is indigenous

ruby plums, cherries, a ripe melon
nectars tease the air
enchant even hummingbird

juniper

she is a mother tree
grown to huge proportions
gnarled roots embed stream's edge
water-sounds skim them like stones

I clear ground of sagebrush
place a bench by the broad trunk
lean back into coarse cool skin
her limbs weave sunlight
blue gin-berries intoxicate the air

this is a place to write poems
to breathe and count my blessings
this is a place my heart knows

high desert air

full, close as ever she comes
the moon seems to speak in tongues
her whispers wake me at dawn

as birds stir
in cool white glow
my soul listens
truth for the taking

a sun-zia crosses blue sky
blesses four directions
in changing light
high desert air

Love quickens
simple hearts
all at once
everywhere

love potion

grazing in cool dawn
two deer in velvet stop
raise magnificent heads
listen near the stream

Love dapples light
on gray cottonwood
colors even my heart lavender

soon enough joy
is next of kin
humming
a mindless tune

grace let loose

el rito veers through river trees
aerates every cell
a sound of play
a feel of grace let loose

ute mountain fills my view
a pyramid of open heart
quickened by the sun
deep in her core a fiery mother
refines the raw stuff of life

compelled towards harmony
as my soul is too, sunning
by a fast moving stream
loving spirit loving me

simple life

lilacs made emily d
smile in her sleeve
in love with a simple life

at this moment
joy seems as sure in me
as the new green of spring

like a pear tree
whose blossoms survive frost
to dream and ripen all summer

all of it is love

morning light teases
cottonwood limbs
curving over the stream

calico cat crouches
in tall summer grasses
waiting a sparrow's distraction

over her shoulder
the pup regards me
then splashes after trout

a good shepherd dog, snoozing
turns an ear to the sound
this texture

hummingbird's fierce defense
butterfly's languid purpose
magpie scolding for
no apparent reason

all of it is love circling home

marvel

we return from city travels
grateful for more time
tending a parcel of earth
by a strong-running stream
generous blue sky reflection

our dogs shadow the woods
on a path to bear canyon
my mare eager to trot uphill
groves of pinon and juniper
give way to aspen and tall pines

we stop in a meadow
such quiet presence
remove our hats
dogs rest, horses graze
simply being
home

winter stream

this dark frozen morning
I can hear the stream
carrying on as if big sun
and breezy leaves are companions

I imagine spotted trout slow
and sleepy, but I chat with them
as I anyway wait for thaw
to make some sense
about the politics of war

a techno-country — mine —
invades the land of milk and honey

we only follow the roman lead
demanding goods and tribute
nothing new at all under the sun

I had such hope for this Age
melding fractured hearts
kind enough to nourish all

so tell me, you must know about these things
how do you float beneath persistent ice
singing songs of love?

chance

because water runs slowly
at the barn my gaze lingers
on tones of mountain color

aspen green flutters near hardy juniper
yet pinon trees stand tannin brown
life ebbed away by drought

is it chance chooses?
breathing is rightly prone
to great fear of losing itself
too soon

anytime is the right time
love something
wild and beautiful

bird fun

while scattering seed for birds
some lines of poetry
circle my mind
just run inside
jot them down
but

a pileated woodpecker
jumps a small feeder
tail feathers wrapped
under swinging thing

blue jays squawk
flutter in mass ascent
a poem
on their wings

ha!
they were only teasing —

so much depends
on red hibiscus
near a calico cat
sunning upside down
in an armchair's lap

magpies

it seems too early
morning barely filters
a canopy of river trees
I hear magpies cajole and stomp
like tibetan monks debating sacred text

nest-building old ways are best
that much they agree but
which tree and how many to begin?

once along the meadow six awkward birds
capped a row of cedar fence posts
my sleek black feline curled on the seventh

she admires them as I do I laughed
their guttural iridescence flashing
but I was not thinking as a cat
she dropped a large glossy kill by the door
wanting in, ears pinned back

a hundred magpies grumbled the roof
I buried the bird with ceremony
still the flock did not disperse until dusk

for days black cat worried an armchair
while I wondered why beauty
needs killing to be prized?

snow dance

in the west heavy with delay
purple clouds promise abundance
crows hurry somewhere seed in cheek
everyone is waiting

two hawks sit posts
near a tree bent red
with gone-by apples
horses paw at roots
dry mute winter earth

brave shafts of light
cleave thunderheads
sweep foothills golden-hearted
still the snows do not descend
breathing small bright songs

but any day now
when the spirit moves
pueblo people will rattle dance
smile in their blankets
as snows come and come
called in the old ways
sure of love

spring

last of the lilacs
tease morning air
languid and serene

meanwhile orange poppies
gather themselves
for a flagrant display

brazen weeds saunter
from ground cover
but I have my eye on them

huge heads of mullein appear
across some barren earth
claiming slim moisture
until blessed thistle moves in

it seems all of a plan
not of my doing — perhaps
I need only (tend the weeds
and) listen to life growing?

owl

at dusk
I was on my way
to feed the horses
when fluttering
took a branch of pinon tree

pygmy owl perched at the crown
shifting feet as I stared
barred yellow coat so fine

my mare kicked the rails for hay
I must have blinked
magic vanished like a rabbit in sage

guests

wild creatures stalk the stream at night
my cats growl at the windows
on a nearby shed I hang a toothy mask
to ward off uninvited guests

a small wooden bridge crosses the water
to a painterly view of ute mountain, stark
pyramid of latent volcano piercing the mesa

I thought it local lore
that spacecraft come there
until one amazing dawn
five golden lights
skimmed the tree line south along the stream
veering suddenly west to vanish near the peak

now these guests are in no way uninvited —
some of us call for intelligent ways out
of the mess we've made of our planet —
I only hope the toothy mask amuses them

seasonal shift

sangre de christo mountains
end of generous monsoon summer
hay fields swirl in golden breeze
aspen leaves tip yellow
a stand of oaks burnt umber

wildflowers bloom innocent
of hard frost due tomorrow
but hummingbirds feed deeply

in this changing beauty
my own aging face seems only
part of nature's seasonal shift
nothing personal as time gone by

yet sap will curl asleep in the roots
more sure than I

neighborhood

a man across the road threatens
to shoot my young dog —
invades his porch most mornings
eats the cat food, pisses on the rail,
teasing a deaf old hound — who knew?

what was I thinking, one hand shielding
sun from my eyes, breathless as she
streaked a quarter mile leaping sagebrush
like a deer, like freedom wild and sure?

now I must contain irrepressible joy
with a radio collar and a fence
really she needs a job
ought to be a ranch hand
circling sheep to a whistle

but she found me
neither young nor wild
mindful to comb my hair
before dinner in town

purgatory

just past the last cold moon
earth devas press spring into reality
sprouting seeds sending shoots
through crusty soil — late snow
blows in from the north
silencing birds mid-song

enough flannel shirts red wooly socks!
I am eyeing the ground
of my summer salad garden
corners crooked with ice

enough last summer's hay!
the horses stomp hooves
slant their eyes at me
as if I took away
yesterday

the fickle end of winter
is a purgatory of impatience
yet none of us can resist
the pull of the moon
stealthy as a cat
sap gains the branches
imagines green

o shaman — a question

as first light breaks on an eastern ridge
mist fringes taos mountain
soon it conspires with a snow-cloud
engulfs the great range, vanishing it

even so
I am standing by a window
sipping morning light when
jackrabbit fills my view
bounding up the drive

he leaps a fence, vanishes
from coyote's eye just as coyote
skids to a stop at my door
hunches down, eyeballs me

I feel like the lead in a southwest novel
sideways glimpsing magic layers
infuse my routine one

I would turn and ask the shaman
if I could — what is this need
to believe
my world is the only one
doing
in a universe
performing such sleights of hand?

blue heeler

wily dog is herding me about
as though I'm her favorite cow
gets me finally to let her out

runs circles in moonlight
yips at bear and coyote
really big trouble

short tail proud
trots back in
but wait

you forgot
good-girl-treats

dusk

in the silence of dusk
I can hear the stream
clearly boisterous
beneath ice

perhaps in the day
sunlight distracts me
shadows on tree limbs
fluctuate like butterflies born

o this is a precious earth
all I know of paradise
is rooted in Breath
eternally passing downstream

rainbow

in the heart of a meadow
kind attributes are kin
something like rainbow
color and sound

lavender gratitude hums
nothing in particular
about most everything

generosity laughs orange
sings baritone snips of arias
cupping one ear the better to hear

sandalwood-scented blue compassion
chants the aum weaving souls

what of love? I cannot live well
without the golden feel of it
flirting my heart tenderly

common tongue

wind culls tired branches
howls like a hungry cat

nostrils flared my mare
paws promises coming green

they speak a common tongue
spring wind, horse heart
first root of soul

yin yang

I shape vessels, harden them in fire
plant seeds and water those
then eat the leaves in earthen bowls

fragile as ozone
tenacious as love
harmony can not be otherwise

peace of heart

kindness laps the edges of my mind
soft eyes, soft world
peace of heart flourishes
among flowers and bees

a summer meadow calls
my body — sit
breathe with the Mother

you have nothing to lose
but the restless foot of time
tapping to be elsewhere

weather

a morning after spring snow
seven doves shake the crest of a juniper
dropping gobs of white on my gray cat
hunched like a rock by their suet

floes break apart releasing run-off
time to trim river trees and wild roses
last season thickets thickened overnight

mountain mystery turns mist
fog, sudden hail, deep sun calling
a sea of red buds across the mesa

in the middle

Love is a blessing with no disguise
stars brighten the sky like joy
brightens an eye or good feelings
take hold of a body and shimmy

the matrix is alive
in a grain of sand
or a drop of water

call on Love and feel
how you stand
in the middle

the sea

these mountains dare my courage
but yearning still
my eyes gaze further west
warm chinook wind
brushes my skin
I can almost feel ocean waves
sound the Mother's heartbeat

I was born by the sea
at night deep fog horns
softly shook my bones
salty air washed over me

some quality of inner light
thrives in me by the sea
green and translucent
as a mermaid's fin

love song

schooled poets are often boxed, yes
while free verse is from a nether world
unfettered by ivory
a wild female plays
absorbing dazzle
rounds her lips
lets loose
a lusty blow of breath
a whalesong of infinity

bones quiver and blood
leaps across common sense —
you see love
requires falling into
heart first or feet first

the head is never in charge
let it sit on the beach and tally waves
while otters squeal and chase

part two

another love

the glance

love awakens
sees itself
in another's eyes

the other awakens
sees love
in reflection

between souls a dance
of eternal magnitude
begins with just this glance

it cannot be contrived
embraced love shares itself
it moves in sudden grace

soft welcome

love rides
a wind of possibility
chance looks twice
quivering

the river holds her ground
only soul-fire glances
let illusion drift away

hold what is precious
against your cheek
listen
soft welcome
stirs your heart

bright light

soul mate
I called her
in the dreamy after
who am I to feel
so cherished

it is only that
an impulse
cast bright light
and I followed

I sensed we were kin
the rhythms of our dance
ancient, honest
learned by heart
called by soul

a curve of clear water

sun-silver on the move
through willows
a sureness runs west
strumming the ground
beneath my lap
love is like that

rushing with birds
a curve of clear water
tumbles the rocks
opens my heart
just like that

delicate

in the morning-cool garden
bird baths reflect a shimmering sky

floating rose petals trace
a scent so delicate
it is more an infusion of light

like the comfort
of my lover's touch
lingering in my hair

simple magic

through the day
I watch my lover's hands
shape kindness from thin air
scattering seed for birds
gentling a horse's mane or
freeing a chipmunk the cat brought in

later they come to me
a loving touch
is simple magic to a body
blossoms a fruit of truth

we are not bound
to suffer for each other
and call it love
as if God hasn't given enough

aloha

fragrant plumeria lei
askew across your brown bosom
pressed against my own

hot sounds of sun on sea
the clatter of shell and stone
seduced by tidal rhythms

heart beat promises
cross my tongue

listening

I sit beneath an elder Juniper
eyes closed, listening

stream's joy flows over stones
nearby my love walks the woods
splendid with dogs and cats
following the lilt of her voice

a sudden chilly gust scatters leaves
my shoes feel too thin

what am I to do?
nothing keeps life from
passing downstream
not even finally loving it

how does hummingbird do it —
sip the flower's beauty
no questions asked?

joy

something
spirals my heart

patterns of light
awaken senses
most aware of beauty

huge floes of ice chime
shifting downstream

caught branches form pools
laced with riotous pebbles
feathery greens, and see

how butterflies hover
near her shoulder
when I catch my lover's eye

charms

Love wears easily
passionate red
dusty rose
or tawny gold

despite her charms I often forget
to add a pinch to the soup
or catch a flash of child-laugh

this, even though I suspect
Love is an all day affair

how my feet wait at the grocers
behind an elder counting change
seems to linger in night air

paradise

red flowers
draw hummingbirds
simply

paradise
sipped
as it was meant to be

a full moon blooming
scatters petals
across my heart

galloping
I scan the horizon
scent of sage underfoot

skin

Love after all is like a mother
pushing her young to surface
to breathe of this world

the unknown keeps me shy
cool air caressing my skin
but once I feel it I leap

the sea of intimacy cocoons
a willingness to change
to breach the surface

to fly
an eternity of sky
to dance for the beloved

tender

excited as meadowlark reaching a note
first rays of light shimmer pearls
on snowy truchas peaks

a soft morning breeze carries
stray song, stirs my gratitude
how our lives entwine love
tender as a downy feather
a crocus, a curled fiddlehead fern

western plains dazzle golden
quite pleased with themselves
meadowlarks crescendo

pleasure

still we lose ourselves in each other
tracing familiar contours

it amazes me the eloquence
of limbs, receptive skin

seems such a simple gift
the dance and fit of us

yet it is an ease hard won
from thoughts
reluctant to surrender
a certain vigilance

love

love
in this present moment
moves moon faintly away

night surrenders
to songbirds as
lilacs untwirl
their scent upon the air

my lover years younger smiles
from a photo, and I grin
still warm in last night's romance
her scent upon my skin

love
how it untwirls me
like the sun

iridescence

an iridescent sea rolls to shore
paintbrush in hand my lover
splashes color onto paper

waves smash green against the coast
shape around boulders made eons ago
lava flowing hot off the mother's tongue

the ocean pulls back into herself
rushing through tribes of pebbles
who sing, tumbled and caressed

nothing to do
but love my life

bliss

when love has had her fill
of passionate embrace

I wander outdoors
to gaze at flowers
and walk the dogs

joy hums along
the open pathways
tree dog bird woman
stream-song happiness

younger

spring snow stampedes
across greening sage
early daffodils faint
I clip the bent stems
yellow revives in a blue vase

this moon pulls life
from roots sleepy yet
stirring in moist earth

in kind my love and I
flirting, skip dinner tonight

curly-haired nubile youth
kisses my cheeks younger

tracks

I seek something in the quiet dark
before my lover stirs
leave lamps unlit
listen as molecules sing
the exquisite brightening of morning

Love makes fine tracks through snow
like galloping horses do
moments before they leap

part three

wild solitude

full moon taos

pearl halo presence
soothing a cobalt dawn
moon mother whispers through trees

men send machines to take my measure
don't they know? I am
the inscrutable Womb
rhythms of ocean tides and soul love

how fortunate
to be born female
a moon in the belly
sensual resonance
ripening potent dreams

stand barefoot to earth
listen for streams running
deeper in the woods

isn't it the same

I can chant mindfully
a hundred names for Love
or simply smile at everyone

isn't it the same
nodding to Breath itself
or to my neighbor
who is breathing?

right before my eyes
the sky streaks orange
captivates my heart

latir

my hands groom the mane
of an ordinary life
my feet stride land
bordering wildness

sometimes double rainbows
crest bear canyon
a certain slant of mist and light

the Mother's heartbeat
a dream of grace
touches this place

déjà vu

we crossed deep waters of the south fork
the mare's hooves rang in my chest as if
I too were ground beneath the river

her hind kept us from washing downstream
while forelegs plunged through braided currents

canyon echoes
traced in that crossing
some other

a moment of fierce breath
bonding every fiber to earth
claiming Her true mother

bosque del apache

circles of them flock
calling to each other
before a mass ascent

in spirals of prairie wind
they turn a double helix
then vanish into infinity

sure of themselves
sand hill cranes
guardians of a particular
hum of universal Love

they reassure me

riding after hummingbird

trapped in a shed hummingbird
beats against implacable glass
faints in my cupped hands
what magnificence, such detail of the eye
beauty blinks, flees the open door

later trotting horses on a mesa trail
indian paintbrush clusters red
as that ruby-throated hummer

a small herd of mule deer chances
from an arroyo, startles into stride

nostrils flared we canter together
thickets of pungent sage, kin
cross-species breathing hard

as they vanish
my lover's laughter
flutters on a breeze

persona

if I could retrieve
original raw substance
persona unshaped
by culture's rasp

would I find also
a shadow-scent
like honeysuckle
drifting in night air?

curious I hover
above a landscape
lush, textured, ripe

I shape myself
a wee bit more
wild-woman sound

ride a red mare bareback
jump this new moon
voice bright

feral

original nature reclaims
what was lost to civilization

as in years later vines
overrun a landscape
logged of its trees and

pottery shards weather
releasing elements
back to earth

still, we know so little —

some zuni call themselves
the lost japanese, their
kachinas dance on stilts
shadows long in the fire
like a good kabuki

one of the tribe found by chance
locked behind glass, totems
needed for puberty rites
incomplete a hundred years

what will you do with them
the museum rung its hands
they are safe here with us

the native smiled broadly now

carved wooden rain gods dissolve
in the very blessing they invoke
mustangs run wild in a west wind

keep my eye

if I am to keep my eye on the divine
should I not read the news?
we disregard great teachers
call Nature our own to reshape

what is this chaos of free will?
perhaps it was granted to the wrong species
or would such power corrupt even butterflies?

so when I do read the news I pray that
light and loving kindness are true selves
soon to reveal the world awake in its own beauty

aloof

gaining a palette of sky at dawn
blue mist steams from the earth
gentling the sharp cold peaks —
mount blanca yet in shadow
silent, aloof, shut to the world
like a hardness in my mind

Light bides her time
unperturbed by transition
sure of high noon as true love

the nature within is free
to say and shape its joy
no matter the season

give the mare her head
she knows a path
through the woods
that opens in to brilliance

split second

it's a beautiful day I notice
nearly missing it
tangled in some fragment
spinning my mind

three stories down
is a warehouse of looms
all lined up repeating
he said she said wish I'd said

if I could shut the door
where would I be?

for a split second I float in peace
my back surrendered to the sea
ears just below the surface

I wonder how many
split seconds it takes
to float like a hundredth monkey?

intimacy

like someone dying
I fell in love today
with a gossamer self

I wept
unnerved
by such clear intimacy

not lost after all
a shade warms her hands
by my fire

upstream

courage
opens to possibility
other than a tangled
probable at hand

it is never too late
love repeats itself
it is never too late

invite beneficence
upstream
golden presence
filament of dreams

invest breath
as if it is possible

amazonia

sturdy legs she's got
and a good eye
looks out for me
stands up for me

strong horsewoman
here in my heart
that's what

bold flexed aligned
with a full moon

solstice

solstice come and gone
still the branches shimmer
smoke-curls linger
in some ancient land

we had a party with the gals
drummed rattled howled
the light within
the light without
our dreams took shape
danced in fire's life

today break ice for the horses
starlight braids their manes
mythic wind gallops their hearts
like thunder across the mesa

solitude

my perfect solitude limits
only the sound of engines
nothing personal

lettuce onion peas and chard
all breezy giddy-giddy
what pleasure gathers dinner
no motoring to town

love finds me home
riding horseback up
and down a mountain
seeing

all that I truly am
sustained
like lilies
like sparrows

curious

hang out with them long enough
and plants speak as I garden —
have I become part of the scenery?

it has come upon me gradually
as vines climb river trees
life unfolds innately curious
what comes next follows
what came before nothing more

to the plants it seems plain
geometry is, beauty is
this universe spirals
a grand rainbow symphony

sense of place

I see them everywhere
bone-white twists of wood
heads raised as if hissing
listen, it is time

so I sit by a smooth-faced rock
toss blue corn and wait
raven jumps a branch calling
juniper pollen sifts through morning

rooting in earth I accept water, minerals
and a touch of bird feet in my hair

sweet sense of place
how I have wondered
now here I sit taking up space

is it kind?

faults in stone fracture
deception fragments

what is real is the present
breath — is it kind?

rays of light from
the heart's inner core
quicken the moment

that's how I'll know

new map

I looked on the new map for tibet
it said china in boldest red

beneath, enclosed in small black brackets
was the name of the land
where Love rings bells
for all sentient beings

"free tibet!" came of age as I did
while her people fell to pogroms

now here in my high desert neighborhood
Love thrives in a small painted stupa
prayer flags dance between trees
welcome devas and bodhisattvas

butterfly fans her wings
unseen wind sounds a bell
encircles the earth
your brave compassionate hand

openly beneficent

the sigh of treetops
this breezy day
informs my heart
with generosity

the letting out
and letting in of love

we risk our lives for it
as we should
and only for love

let it color my world
joy and affection
all sentient beings
openly beneficent

change

redwing blackbird tops a juniper
officially declares spring in the rockies

 yet weather, politics, necessary
spiritual growth are undetermined

rolls of bitter wind raise dust devils
spinning thin soil across the mesa

a most difficult task stares in my face
no matter the outcome
welcome the bringer of change

spring run-off

a sage-scented ruff
quietly parts tall grasses
coyote-eyes glint
like mica in red earth
sorrel mares race mesa wind
shadows long in moonlight

beneath the meadow
ancient boulders dream
bones of the Mother hold
all our roots among them
it has been this way a long time

meanwhile we sleep in our beds
jaws slack, believing
we have tamed fire

Nature survives our human conceit
a great arm of kali
spring run-off
sweeps away shallow roots
starts a new day

forgive

laughter pierces me
tenderly fills the cavities
those places holding silence
where only sadness would be told

tendrils decorate tombs
marigolds dust my face
like a picnic with ancestors
autumn day of the dead

so much theatre haunts my past
forgive, and choose again
brilliance of heart

I think finally
love like a rainbow
is all I am here to do

a moment

I became gradually aware
stroking a cat curled in my lap

together we listened
beyond the stream
to whatever it is

weaves an entire fabric
loving the universe
right back

champagne

one could do worse than
make art without asking why
make love empty of time

sit by a river breathing
a lot of dream happens
while trout swim upstream

good weather
plentiful foods
world peace

my soul sips champagne

a bell

counting inequities
forget about it

so much sand beneath your feet
slows your way to solid ground

call for Love again
like a bell sounding in thick fog

in the long and the short
of this beautiful
inexplicably cruel world

isn't Love all
that can possibly matter?

Acknowledgements

A special thank you to Connie King. She is not only the book's designer, but also poetry editor and publishing consultant. Her gracious mentoring shaped concept into reality.

Thank you also to Ellen McNeilly, Karen Waller, and Jolly Smith for reading and consultation on parts of the manuscript in progress. I am grateful as well to the many Preview readers who offered thoughtful commentary and response to a selection of poems. It so encouraged me to add one more voice for love to the world's song.

About the author

Lorraine Lipani grew up in Brooklyn, New York, b. 1949. She attended SUNY Oneonta during the innovative 1960s. While earning a Liberal Arts degree in Literature, she realized a passion for writing and art-making, as well as Jungian psychology and mysticism. In her twenties, she worked at The Edgar Cayce Foundation in Virginia, trained there as a massage therapist, and maintained a practice for over forty years. In her thirties she studied ceramics and has kept an art studio ever since. In her forties, she learned how to ride a horse, her second favorite relationship. Lorraine and her lover, artist Jolly Smith, lived in northern New Mexico for many years before moving to The Sea Ranch, California in 2013—still riding horses in beautiful places.

www.ingramcontent.com/pod-product-compliance
Lightning Source LLC
Chambersburg PA
CBHW021127300426
44113CB00006B/316